Vibrant Carou

© Paula Puddephatt, 2020

Paula Writes:

paulathewriter.com

Dreams and Illusions

coloured lights
swirling
through her mind
tonight
splashes of vibrant
paint upon the night sky
upon a canvas of ebony
a night filled with dreams and illusions
which dissolve into
darkness
pure darkness and delusions
obsessions and confusion
swirling whirling
coloured lights
that dance through her mind
tonight

Spiritual Peace

I find my place of spiritual peace
Again, just when I feel I never will.
There is a sense of freedom and release.
I can't know all the answers, but am still

In touch with *The Divine*, and that is real.
We're all connected. Life is precious, and
Life doesn't end with death. Sometimes we feel
A presence, and we come to understand

That nobody who's ever been has gone.
The spirits of the ones we've loved remain.
They will protect us - help us to go on.
There is almost a beauty in the pain.

Although sometimes I find it hard to trust,
Truth's constant. Feel the patterns in the rust.

Reflections

Precious time for peace
and healing:

time to clearly see

the subtle shading,
never visible
to the
naked human eye.

Reflected in this ancient mirror,
what we gradually
start to see
are:
the hidden pastel textures,
connecting us
to *The Divine*.

Lime Trees

Summers consist of
peridot mornings,
and emerald afternoons.
The trees filter the sunlight -
so often saving me from
those headaches, which might have
mutated, evolved into migraines.

By autumn, the leaves have changed colour:
a poet's palette of
amber, copper,
gold and red.

In winter, the trees are slender,
with a stark, grey-brown beauty:
looking fragile,
yet able to endure
the harsh frosts of the season.

And, throughout the seasons,
"they" plot.
They want
a concrete universe,
so they mark out their potential
victims, with orange spots.

The letters to local residents are headed:
"Implementation of
Environmental Improvements".

Yet, trees can bleed.
Scenes of carnage seal the deal.
They win; we lose.
So much wildlife, instantly evicted.

Fluorescent yellow workmen circle tree stumps,
inspecting their day's work -
before going for "a pint",
and home for tea.

Spring is cancelled.

Dreams

collage of dreams
memories framed
in mahogany

silent symphony
of vibrant darkness

Carousel

around and around
on the carousel
spinning
around and around
merry-go-round
multi-coloured dreams
vibrant darkness
the colours of confusion
around and around
the endless circles
cycles
horses longing for
the wild
longing to run
far away
leave this fairground ride
of psychedelic craziness
behind
to feel their manes caressing the wind
their spirits embracing the speed
the freedom
around and around
endless cycles
on the carousel of dreams

Girl in Pink

swirling girl
in pretty pink
and blue denim

the years lie ahead for you
stretched out like vast fields
of potential daisy chains

don't let this world break you
don't let them take away
your spirit
your pride

Dreaming in Neon

dreaming in neon
beneath star-filled skies
of indigo velvet

Evening Stillness

The stillness in *near silence*
is the gift of solitude.
I tentatively reach out
and touch
the steel-clad wings
of angels.
The sky is quietly glorious
in shades of gold, peach, lavender.
Another day accomplished. I am glad to be
alive.

The Legend of Lucy Lightfoot

At seventeen, so radiant,
hair raven black, eyes emerald green -
the local lads, they just don't stand a chance.
Lucy's heart is in the village church -
the love of her life, a wooden effigy,
of a soldier who died long ago,
before Lucy's birth.

She has visited the tomb
every day since she was twelve.
She brings her lover flowers,
tells him details of
her daily life:
living on a local farm,
with her father and two brothers.

Then, one day, Lucy is riding
her beloved white horse,
in the direction of the little church.
She gets caught in a storm,
so fierce. The skies turn black.
She must reach the church,
her sanctuary from the violence
of the elements.
She tethers her terrified horse
to the rusty gate,
and soon she is safe, with her lover again.

Lucy's horse was later discovered,
frightened and alone.
But where did *Lucy* go?
No trace of Lucy Lightfoot was ever found -
although...

Only The Horse

There was an eclipse,
and a violent storm, on the afternoon
that Lucy Lightfoot disappeared.
Only Lucy's horse ever saw
the white light,
as lightning struck the steeple
of the little church.
He was tethered
to the rusty gate -
and, of course, the poor animal was afraid.
Lucy was inside the church -
by her lover's side.
Her lover - from a former life.
She had visited his tomb
each day since she was twelve,
presenting flowers, whispering secrets
and words of passion,
to his wooden effigy.
She must have realised
that the time was right,
that she and her valiant soldier
would finally reunite.
But only the horse ever saw
the white light -
and no trace of Lucy Lightfoot
was found, beyond that afternoon.

Pastel Shades

Hope sometimes comes to us
in pastel shades.
It isn't always
either
black or white,
or even grey.
I feel that hope,
when needed most,
will often be
revealed in
pastel shades.